WORSHIP SONGS
❋ FOR ❋
UKULELE

ISBN 978-1-4584-1528-8

HAL•LEONARD®
CORPORATION

7777 W. BLUEMOUND RD. P.O. BOX 13819 MILWAUKEE, WI 53213

Visit Hal Leonard Online at
www.halleonard.com

CONTENTS

Amazing Grace

(My Chains Are Gone)

Words by John Newton
Traditional American Melody
Additional Words and Music by Chris Tomlin and Louie Giglio

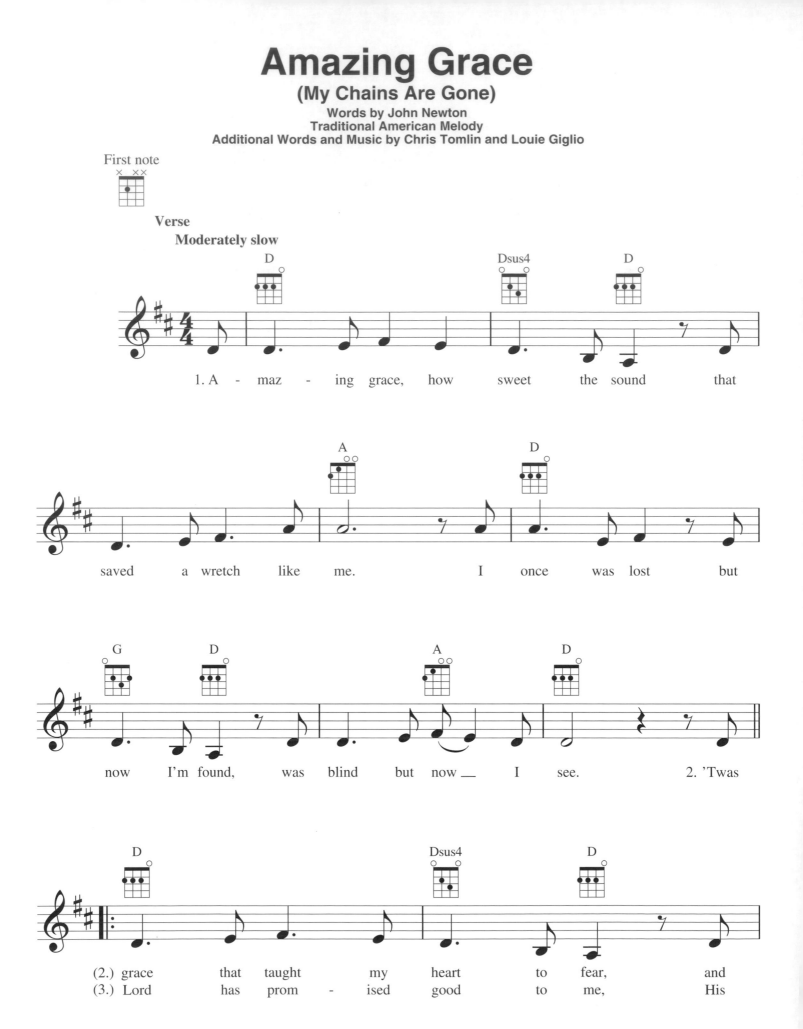

grace   my fears   re - lieved.   How pre - cious did   that
Word   my hope   se - cures.   He   will   my shield and

grace   ap - pear   the   hour   I   first _____ be -
por - tion be   as   long   as   life _____ en -

%: Chorus

lieved. }
dures. }   My   chains are   gone,   I've been set

free.   My   God, my   Sav - ior _____ has ran - somed

me.   And   like   a   flood, _____ His mer - cy

To Coda

rains   un - end - ing love, ___   a - maz - ing

Blessed Be Your Name

Words and Music by Matt Redman and Beth Redman

-ert place, ___ tho' I walk through ___ the wil -
-fer - ing, ___ tho' there's pain in _____ the of -

- der - ness, ___ bless - ed be Your name. ___
- fer - ing, ___ bless - ed be Your name. ___

Pre-Chorus

Ev - 'ry bless - ing You pour out I'll turn back to

praise. When the dark - ness clos - es in, Lord,

still I will say: Bless - ed be the

𝄋 Chorus

name of _____ the Lord, _____ bless - ed be Your

Come, Now Is the Time to Worship

Words and Music by Brian Doerksen

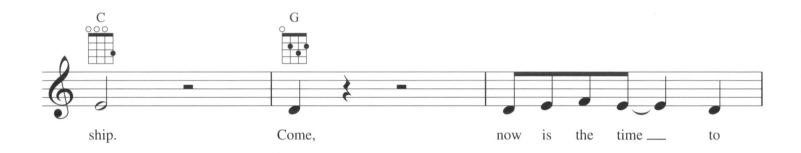

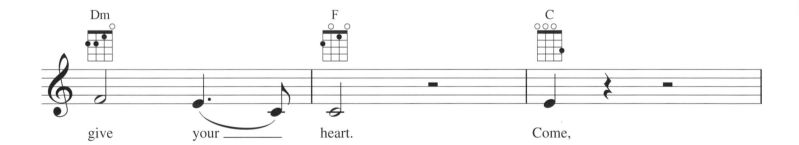

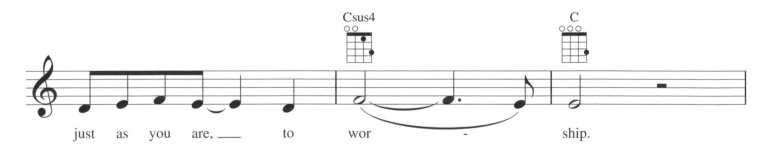

Come,   just as you are, ___ be - fore your ___

God.   Come.

Fine

Chorus

One day ev - 'ry tongue will con - fess ___ You are God, ___

one day ev - 'ry knee ___ will bow. ___

Still, the great - est treas - ure re - mains ___ for those ___ who glad -

D.C. al Fine

- ly choose ___ You now. ___

11

Enough

Words and Music by Chris Tomlin and Louie Giglio

All of You _____ is more than e - nough _

_ for all of me, _____ for _____ ev - 'ry thirst _

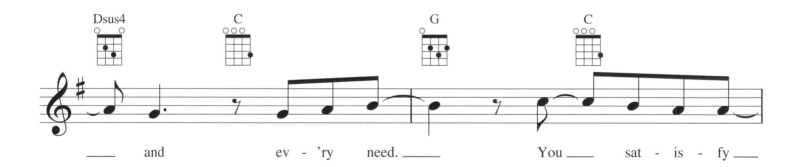

_ and ev - 'ry need. _____ You _____ sat - is - fy _

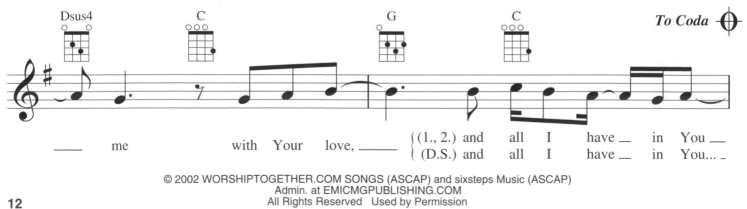

_ me with Your love, _____ {(1., 2.) and all I have _ in You _____
{(D.S.) and all I have _ in You... _

___ is more than e - nough. ___

1. You are my ___ sup - ply, ___
2. You're my sac - ri - fice ___

___ my breath ___ of life, _____ still more awe -
___ of great - est price, _____ still more awe -

- some than I know. _ You are my ___ re - ward, ___
- some than I know. _ You're my com - ing King, ___

___ worth liv - ing for, _____ still more awe -
___ You are ev - 'ry - thing, _____ still more awe -

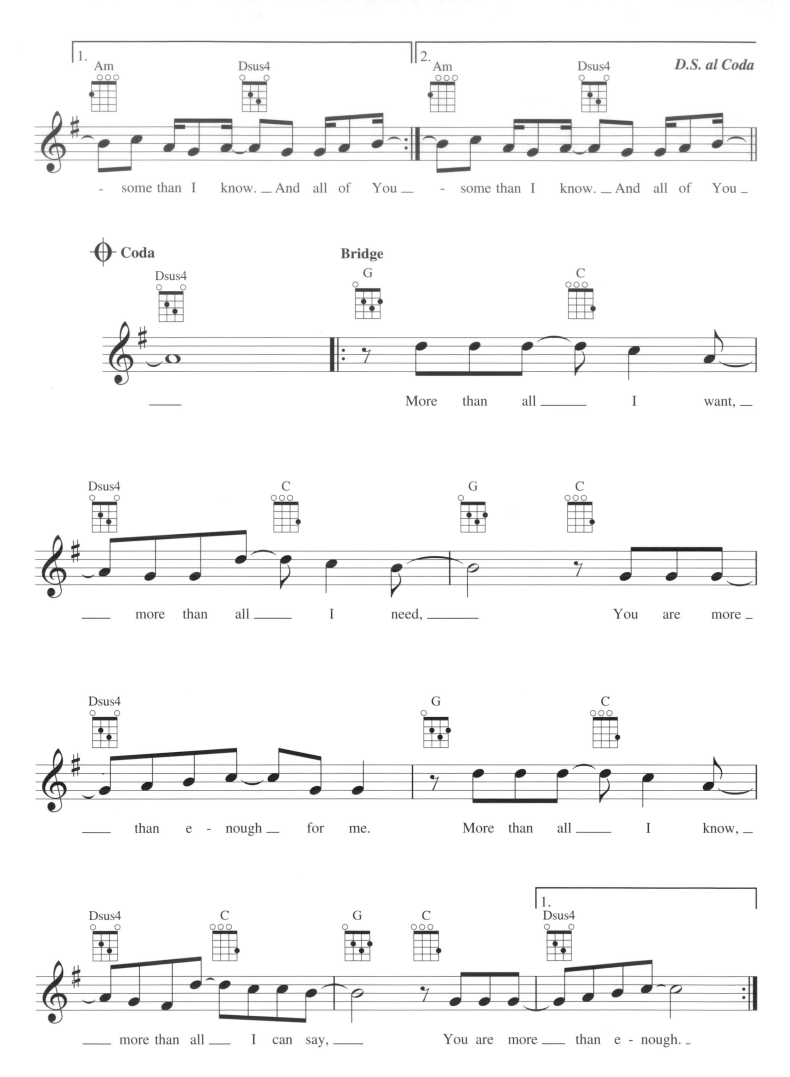

Everyday

Words and Music by Joel Houston

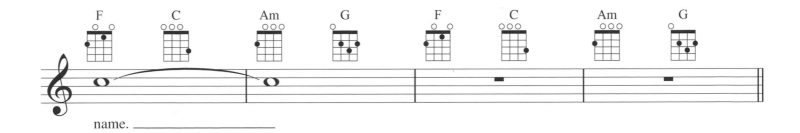

name. _____

Verse

2. Ev - 'ry day, __ Lord, I'll _____ learn to stand __ up - on ___ Your Word. __

____ And I pray __ that I, _____ that I may come __ to know __ You more, __

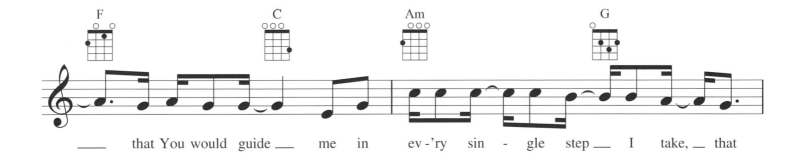

____ that You would guide ___ me in ev - 'ry sin - gle step __ I take, __ that

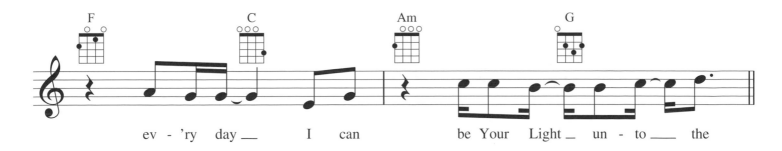

ev - 'ry day __ I can be Your Light __ un - to ___ the

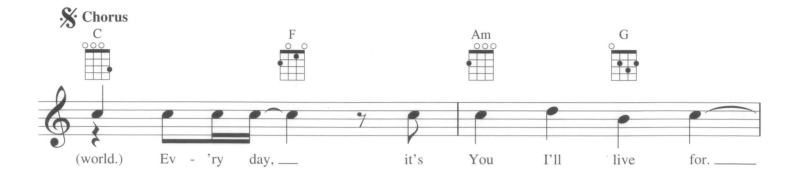

(world.) Ev - 'ry day, ___ it's You I'll live for. ___

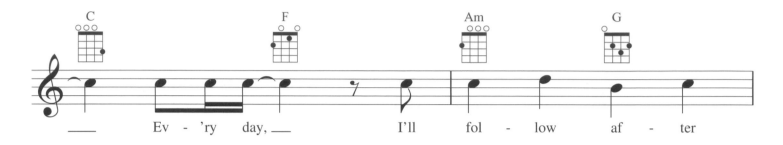

___ Ev - 'ry day, ___ I'll fol - low af - ter

You. Ev - 'ry day, ___ I'll walk with You, my

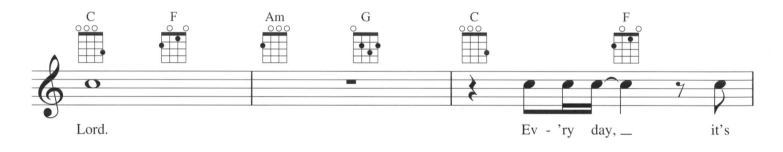

Lord. Ev - 'ry day, ___ it's

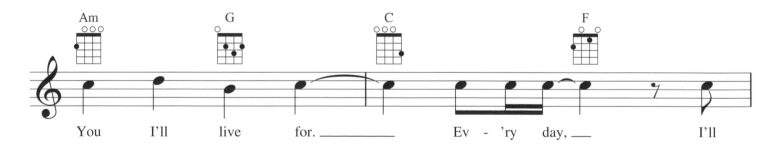

You I'll live for. ___ Ev - 'ry day, ___ I'll

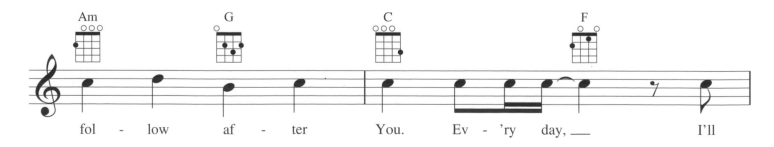

fol - low af - ter You. Ev - 'ry day, ___ I'll

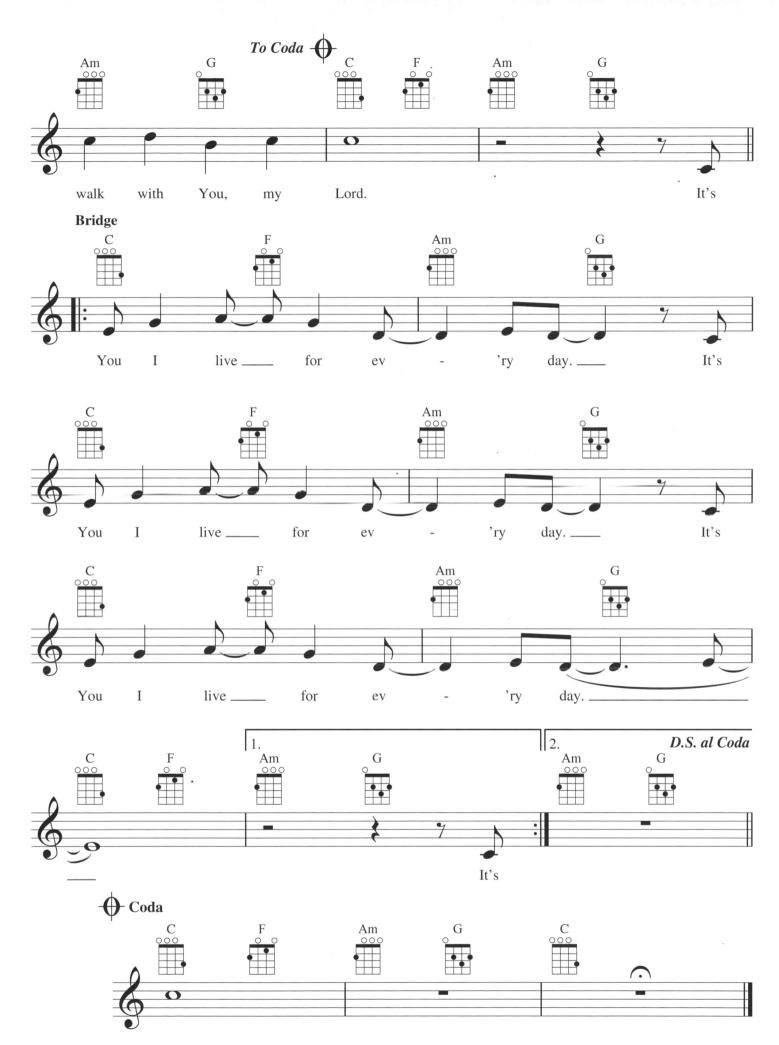

Glory to God Forever

Words and Music by Steve Fee and Vicky Beeching

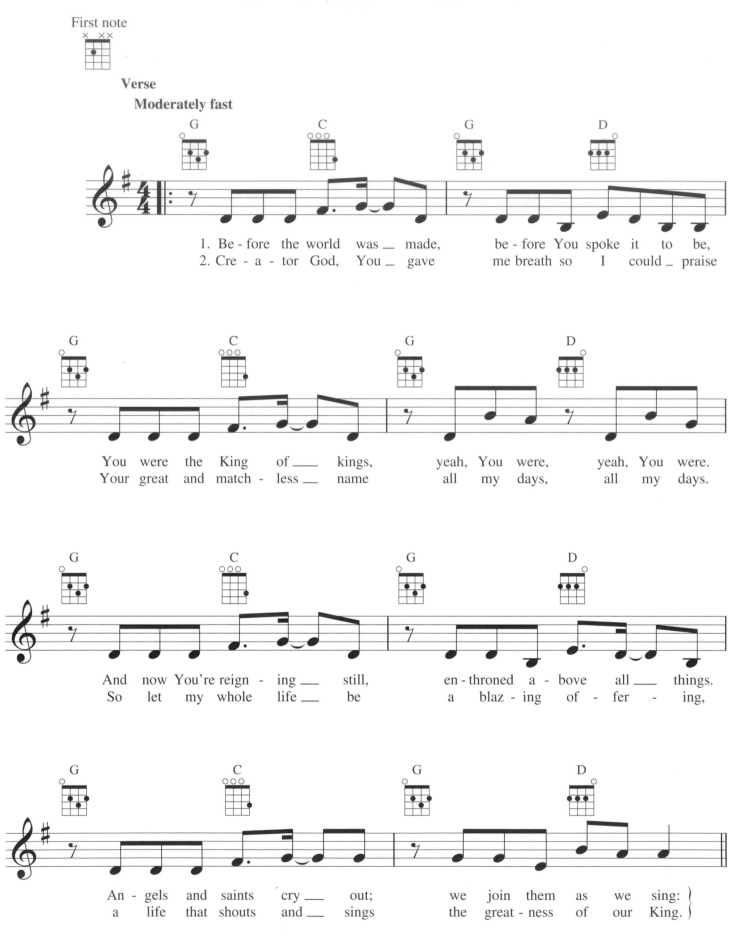

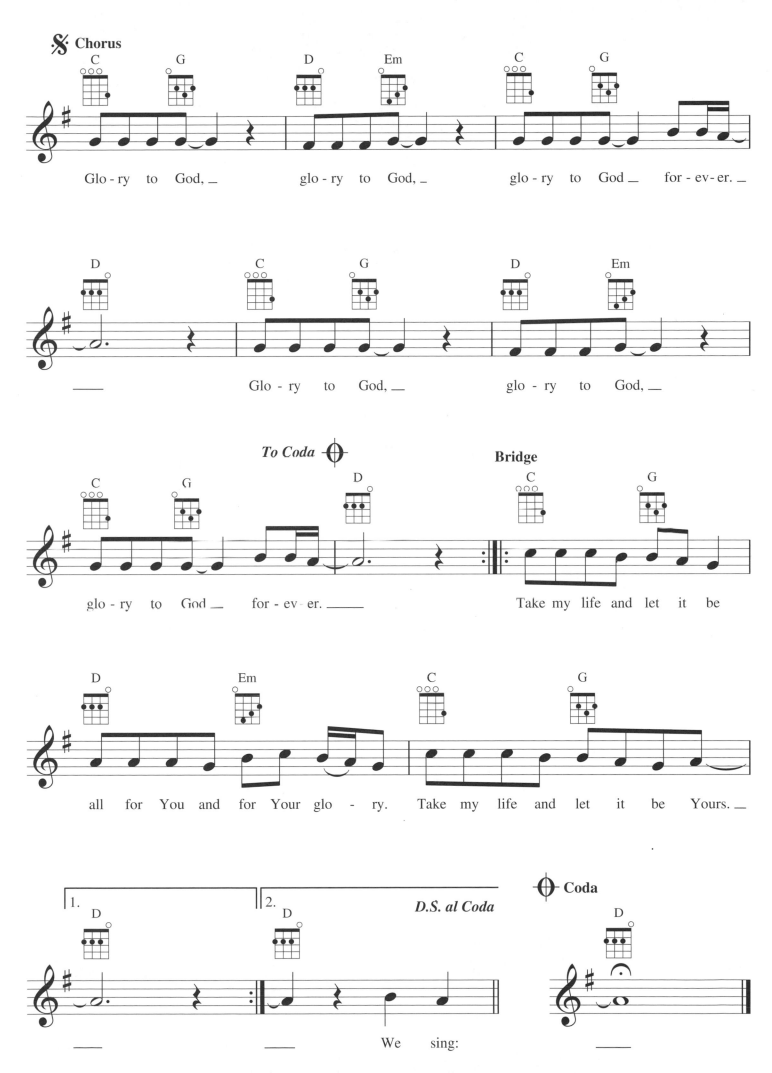

God of Wonders

Words and Music by Marc Byrd and Steve Hindalong

ho - ly. ___ The u - ni - verse ___ de - clares ___ Your maj - es - ty. You are

ho - ly, ___ ho - ly; ___ Lord of heav-en and ___ earth, _

___ Lord of heav - en and ___ earth. ___

Outro

Hal - le - lu - jah ___ to the Lord of ___ heav - en and ___ earth. _

___ Hal - le - lu - jah ___ to the Lord of ___ heav-en and ___ earth. _

___ Hal - le - lu - jah ___ to the Lord of ___ heav-en and ___ earth. ___

Here I Am to Worship

Words and Music by Tim Hughes

wor - thy, al - to - geth - er won - der - ful to me. _____

_____ And I'll nev - er know _ how much _____

_____ it cost _____ to see _____ my sin _____ up - on _____

_____ that cross. _____ And I'll nev - er know _____ how much _____

_____ it cost _____ to see _____ my sin _____ up - on _____ that cross. _____

Here I am to

_____

25

Holy Is the Lord

Words and Music by Chris Tomlin and Louie Giglio

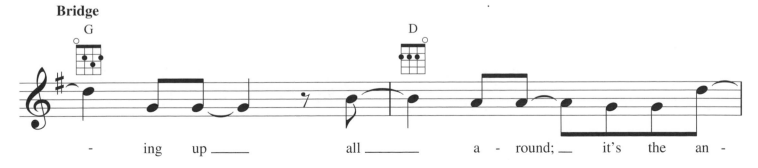

-them of _____ the Lord's _____ re - nown. _____ It's ris -

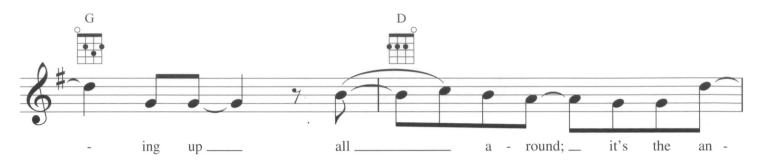

-ing up _____ all _____ a - round; _____ it's the an -

-them of _____ the Lord's _____ re - nown. _____

To - geth - er we _____ sing, _____

and ev - 'ry - one sing:

D.S. al Coda   ⊕ **Coda**

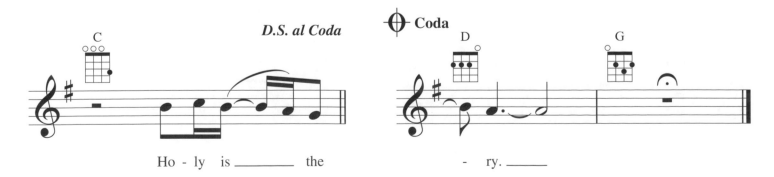

Ho - ly is _____ the   - ry. _____

How Great Is Our God

Words and Music by Chris Tomlin, Jesse Reeves and Ed Cash

It trem - bles at ___ His voice, ___ trem - bles at ___ His voice. ___
the Li - on and ___ the Lamb, ___ Li - on and ___ the Lamb. ___

Chorus
G

How great ___ is our God! ___ Sing with me: ___ How

Em

great is our God! ___ And all ___ will see how great, how great ___

D   G   1.

___ is our God! ___   2. And

2.   **Bridge**
G

Name a - bove ___ all names, ___

Hosanna

(Praise Is Rising)

Words and Music by Paul Baloche and Brenton Brown

who saves us, _____ wor-thy of all _____ our prais - es. _____

Ho - san - na, ho -

san - na. _____ Come have Your way _____

_____ a - mong us. _____ We wel-come You here, _____

_____ Lord Je - sus. _____

Love the Lord

Words and Music by Lincoln Brewster

In Christ Alone

Words and Music by Keith Getty and Stuart Townend

1. In Christ a - lone my hope is found, He is my
(2.) lone, who took on flesh, full - ness of
(3.) ground His bod - y lay, Light of the
(4.) life, no fear in death; this is the

light, my strength, my song. This cor - ner - stone, this sol - id
God in help - less babe! This gift of love and right - eous -
world by dark - ness slain. Then burst - ing forth in glo - rious
pow'r of Christ in me. From life's first cry to fi - nal

ground, firm through the fierc - est drought and
ness, scorned by the ones He came to
day, up from the grave He rose a -
breath, Je - sus com - mands my des - ti -

Chorus

storm. What heights of love, what depths of
save. Till on that cross as Je - sus
gain! And as He stands in vic - to -
ny. No pow'r of hell, no scheme of

peace, when fears are stilled, when striv - ings
died, the wrath of God was sat - is -
ry, sin's curse has lost its grip on
man, can ev - er pluck me from His

cease! My Com - fort - er, my All in All, here in the
fied. For ev - 'ry sin on Him was laid; here in the
me, for I am His and He is mine, bought with the
hand. Till He re - turns or calls me home, here in the

1.–3.

love of Christ I stand. 2. In Christ a -
death of Christ I live. 3. There in the
pre - cious blood of Christ. 4. No guilt in
pow'r of Christ I'll

4. **Outro**

stand. Here in the pow'r of Christ I'll stand!

39

Lord, I Lift Your Name on High

Words and Music by Rick Founds

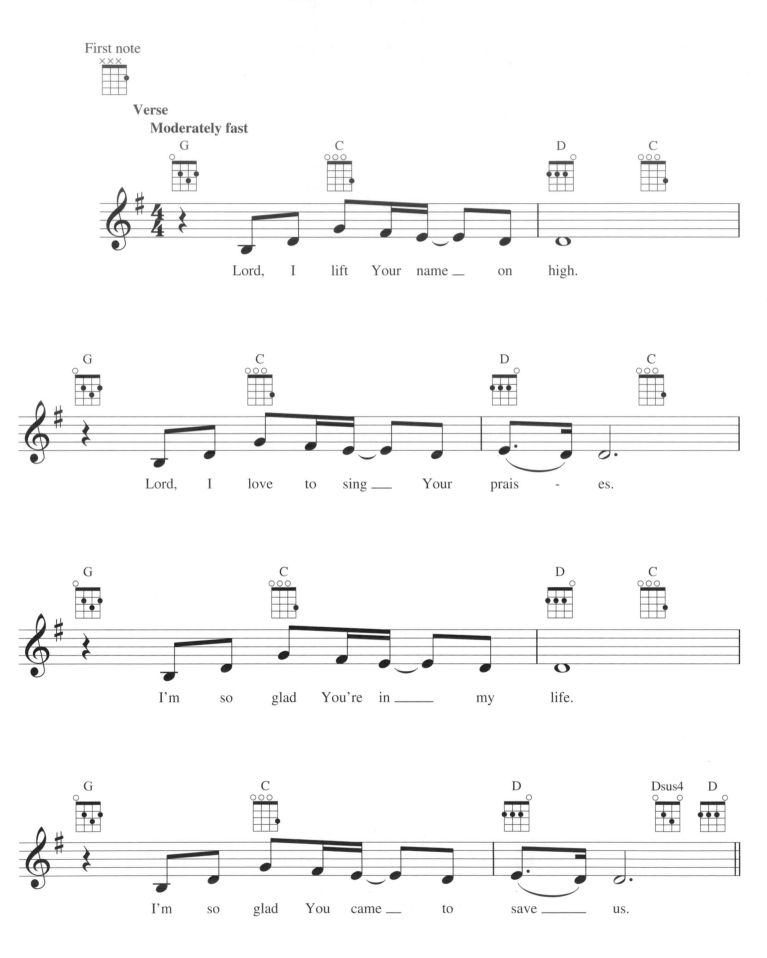

Lord, Reign in Me

Words and Music by Brenton Brown

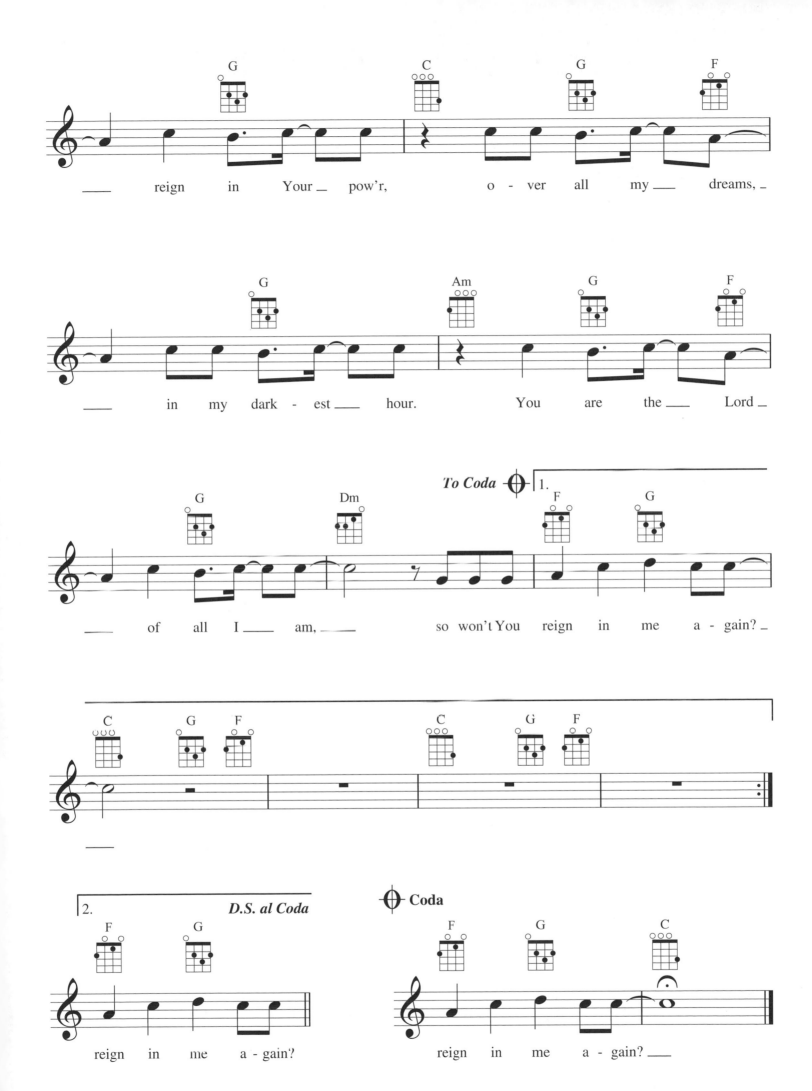

reign in Your pow'r, o - ver all my dreams,

in my dark - est hour. You are the Lord

of all I am, so won't You reign in me a - gain?

reign in me a - gain? reign in me a - gain?

More Precious Than Silver

Words and Music by Lynn DeShazo

First note
×××

Chorus
Moderately

Lord, You are more pre - cious than

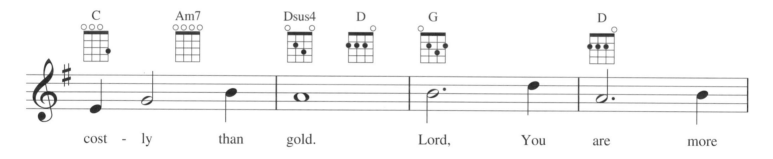

sil - ver. Lord, You are more

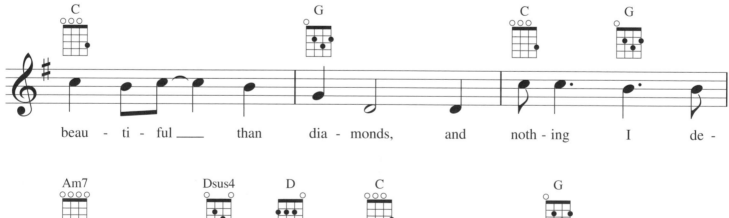

cost - ly than gold. Lord, You are more

beau - ti - ful ___ than dia - monds, and noth - ing I de -

sire com - pares with You. ___

Mighty to Save

Words and Music by Ben Fielding and Reuben Morgan

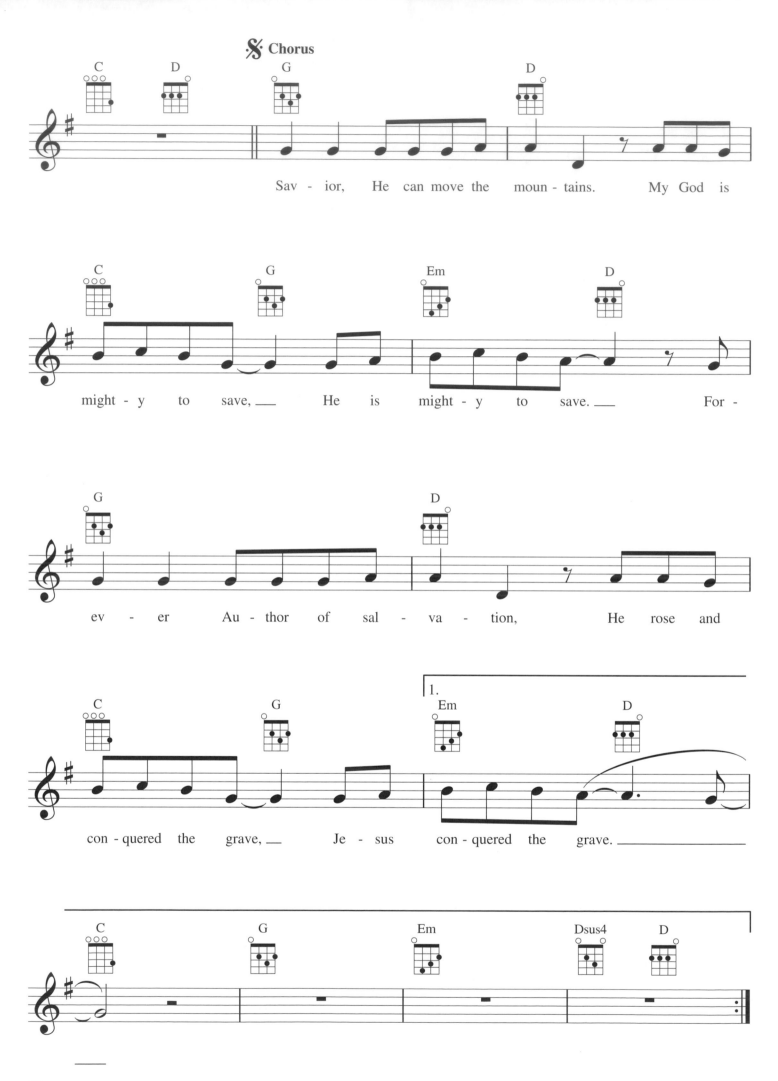

Chorus

Sav - ior, He can move the moun - tains. My God is

might - y to save, ___ He is might - y to save. ___ For -

ev - er Au - thor of sal - va - tion, He rose and

1.

con - quered the grave, ___ Je - sus con - quered the grave. ___

Open the Eyes of My Heart

Words and Music by Paul Baloche

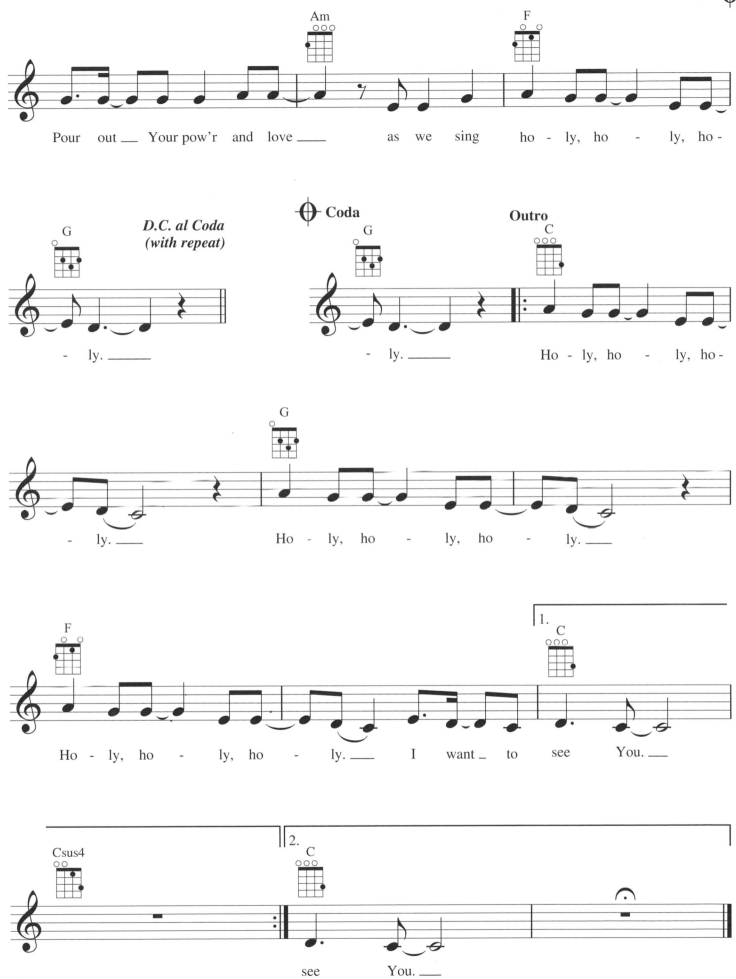

Sing to the King

Words and Music by Billy James Foote

Chorus

Come, let us sing ____ a song, ____ a

song de - clar - ing we ____ be - long ____ to Je - sus,

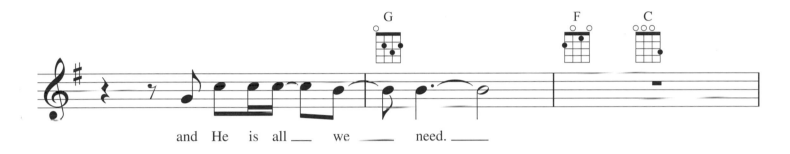

and He is all ____ we ____ need. ____

Lift up a heart ____ of praise. ____ Sing now with voic -

- es raised ____ to Je - sus. Sing to ____ the ____

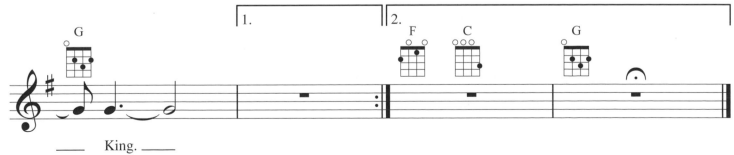

____ King. ____

Step by Step

Words and Music by David Strasser "Beaker"

We Fall Down

Words and Music by Chris Tomlin

There Is Joy in the Lord

Words and Music by Cheri Keaggy

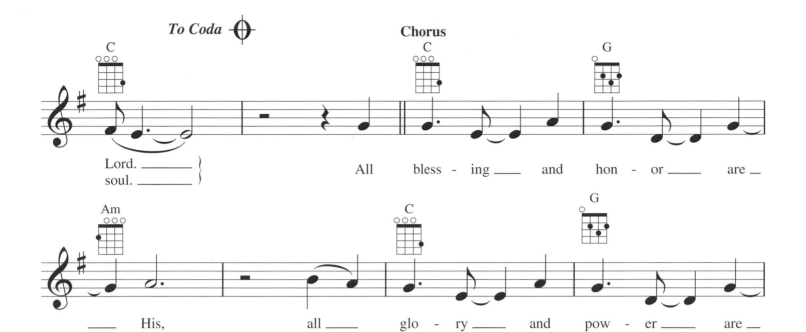

Lord. _____
soul. _____

All bless - ing _____ and hon - or _____ are _____

_____ His, all _____ glo - ry _____ and pow - er _____ are _____

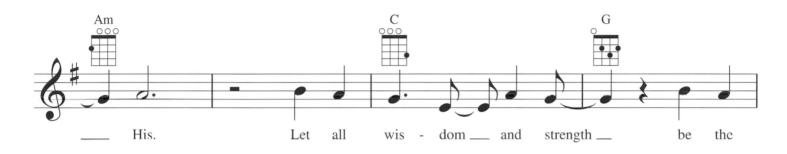

_____ His. Let all wis - dom _____ and strength _____ be the

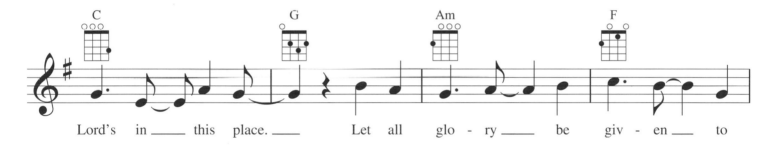

Lord's in _____ this place. _____ Let all glo - ry _____ be giv - en _____ to

Him. There is There is

It's a -

Outro

bound - ing _____ in love to _____ my _____ soul. _____

You Are My King

(Amazing Love)

Words and Music by Billy James Foote

that You, my King, _ would die _ for me? _

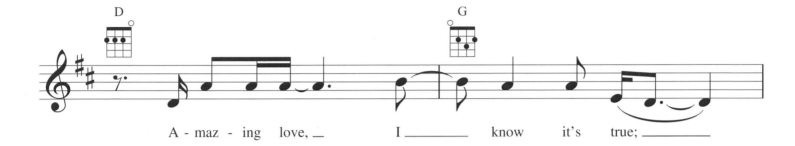

A - maz - ing love, _ I _ know it's true; _

it's my joy _ to hon - or You. _ In all _ I _

To Coda ⊕

Bridge

_ do, _ I hon - or You. _ You are my _

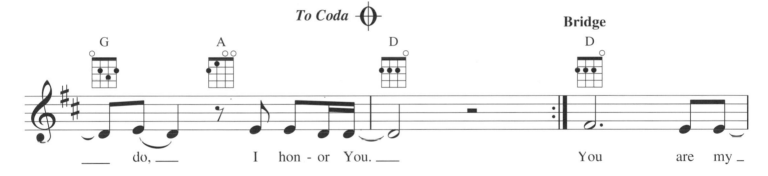

_ King. You are my _ King. Je - sus, You are my _

⊕ **Coda**

D.S. al Coda

_ King. Je - sus, You are my _ King.

_____

You're Worthy of My Praise

Words and Music by David Ruis

all of Your ways (all Your ways).
trust You a - lone (trust in You a - lone).

Chorus

I will give ___ You all my wor - ship,

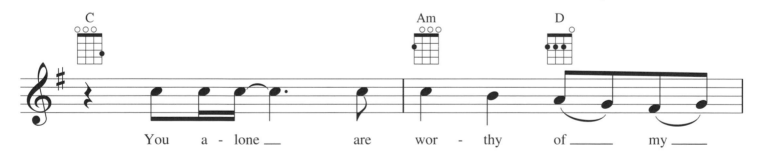

I will give ___ You all my praise. ___

You a - lone ___ I long to wor - ship,

You a - lone ___ are wor - thy of ___ my ___

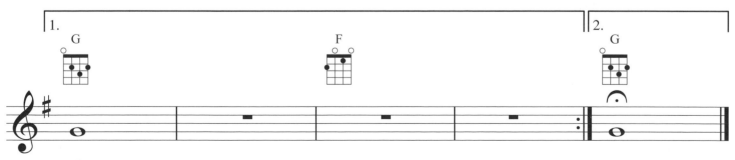

1.
praise.

2.
praise.

You Never Let Go

Words and Music by Matt Redman and Beth Redman

First note

Verse
Moderately

C

1. E - ven though I walk through the val - ley of the
(2.) light that is com - ing for the

shad - ow of death, Your per - fect love is cast - ing out fear.
heart that holds on, a glo - rious light be - yond all com - pare.

And e - ven when I'm caught in the mid - dle of the
And there will be an end to these trou - bles, but un -

storms of this life, I won't turn back; I know You are near. }
til that day comes, we'll live to know You here on the earth. }

HAL•LEONARD®
UKULELE PLAY-ALONG

Now you can play your favorite songs on your uke with great-sounding backing tracks to help you sound like a bona fide pro! The audio also features playback tools so you can adjust the tempo without changing the pitch and loop challenging parts.

HAL•LEONARD®
www.halleonard.com

The Best Collections for Ukulele

The Best Songs Ever

70 songs have now been arranged for ukulele. Includes: Always • Bohemian Rhapsody • Memory • My Favorite Things • Over the Rainbow • Piano Man • What a Wonderful World • Yesterday • You Raise Me Up • and more.
00282413 . . . . $17.99

Campfire Songs for Ukulele

30 favorites to sing as you roast marshmallows and strum your uke around the campfire. Includes: God Bless the U.S.A. • Hallelujah • The House of the Rising Sun • I Walk the Line • Puff the Magic Dragon • Wagon Wheel • You Are My Sunshine • and more.
00129170 . . . . . . $14.99

The Daily Ukulele

arr. Liz and Jim Beloff
Strum a different song everyday with easy arrangements of 365 of your favorite songs in one big songbook! Includes favorites by the Beatles, Beach Boys, and Bob Dylan, folk songs, pop songs, kids' songs, Christmas carols, and Broadway and Hollywood tunes, all with a spiral binding for ease of use.
00240356 Original Edition. $39.99
00240681 Leap Year Edition $39.99
00119270 Portable Edition $37.50

Disney Hits for Ukulele

Play 23 of your favorite Disney songs on your ukulele. Includes: The Bare Necessities • Cruella De Vil • Do You Want to Build a Snowman? • Kiss the Girl • Lava • Let It Go • Once upon a Dream • A Whole New World • and more.
00151250 . . . . . . $16.99

Also available:
00291547 **Disney Fun Songs for Ukulele** . . . $16.99
00701708 **Disney Songs for Ukulele** $14.99
00334696 **First 50 Disney Songs on Ukulele** . $16.99

First 50 Songs You Should Play on Ukulele

An amazing collec-tion of 50 accessible, must-know favorites: Edelweiss • Hey, Soul Sister • I Walk the Line • I'm Yours • Imagine • Over the Rainbow • Peaceful Easy Feeling • The Rainbow Connection • Riptide • more.
00149250 . . . . $16.99

Also available:
00292082 **First 50 Melodies on Ukulele** . . . $15.99
00289029 **First 50 Songs on Solo Ukulele** . . $15.99
00347437 **First 50 Songs to Strum on Uke** . $16.99

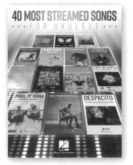

40 Most Streamed Songs for Ukulele

40 top hits that sound great on uke! Includes: Despacito • Feel It Still • Girls like You • Happier • Havana • High Hopes • The Middle • Perfect • 7 Rings • Shallow • Shape of You • Something Just like This • Stay • Sucker • Sunflower • Sweet but Psycho • Thank U, Next • There's Nothing Holdin' Me Back • Without Me • and more!
00298113 . . . . $17.99

The 4 Chord Songbook

With just 4 chords, you can play 50 hot songs on your ukulele! Songs include: Brown Eyed Girl • Do Wah Diddy Diddy • Hey Ya! • Ho Hey • Jessie's Girl • Let It Be • One Love • Stand by Me • Toes • With or Without You • and many more.
00142050 . . . . $16.99

Also available:
00141143 **The 3-Chord Songbook** $16.99

Pop Songs for Kids

30 easy pop favorites for kids to play on uke, including: Brave • Can't Stop the Feeling! • Feel It Still • Fight Song • Happy • Havana • House of Gold • How Far I'll Go • Let It Go • Remember Me (Ernesto de la Cruz) • Rewrite the Stars • Roar • Shake It Off • Story of My Life • What Makes You Beautiful • and more.
00284415 . . . . $16.99

Simple Songs for Ukulele

50 favorites for standard G-C-E-A ukulele tuning, including: All Along the Watchtower • Can't Help Falling in Love • Don't Worry, Be Happy • Ho Hey • I'm Yours • King of the Road • Sweet Home Alabama • You Are My Sunshine • and more.
00156815 . . . . $14.99

Also available:
00276644 **More Simple Songs for Ukulele** . $14.99

Top Hits of 2020

18 uke-friendly tunes of 2020 are featured in this collection of melody, lyric and chord arrangements in standard G-C-E-A tuning. Includes: Adore You (Harry Styles) • Before You Go (Lewis Capaldi) • Cardigan (Taylor Swift) • Daisies (Katy Perry) • I Dare You (Kelly Clarkson) • Level of Concern (twenty one pilots) • No Time to Die (Billie Eilish) • Rain on Me (Lady Gaga feat. Ariana Grande) • Say So (Doja Cat) • and more.
00355553 . . . . $14.99

Also available:
00302274 **Top Hits of 2019** $14.99

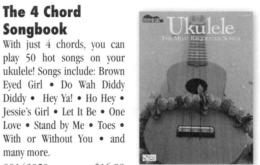

Ukulele: The Most Requested Songs

Strum & Sing Series
Cherry Lane Music
Nearly 50 favorites all expertly arranged for ukulele! Includes: Bubbly • Build Me Up, Buttercup • Cecilia • Georgia on My Mind • Kokomo • L-O-V-E • Your Body Is a Wonderland • and more.
02501453 . . . . $14.99

The Ultimate Ukulele Fake Book

Uke enthusiasts will love this giant, spiral-bound collection of over 400 songs for uke! Includes: Crazy • Dancing Queen • Downtown • Fields of Gold • Happy • Hey Jude • 7 Years • Summertime • Thinking Out Loud • Thriller • Wagon Wheel • and more.
00175500 9" x 12" Edition $45.00
00319997 5.5" x 8.5" Edition $39.99